THE ENLIGHTEN TRUTH

A GLIMPSE OF REALITY

LAKSH WADHWA

Special thanks to a Thought that gave me the motivation
to write

Contents

Preface

The Book came into existence to help the upcoming generation know the reality of the world and about the simulation in which a human is

Table Of Contents

CHAPTER ONE

UNIVERSAL COPIES

THE formation of the universe is one of the biggest mysteries in the world. The universe is highly complex and it's expanding daily. Whereas there is not only one universe present there are several universes. The universe contains multiple complex things like black holes, white holes, etc. There are several theories to prove how the universe was created like the big bang, god, etc. But nobody exactly knows how the universe was created.

Where the explanation of the creation of multiple verses is also very complex.

So if we say that the first universe was created through the process of the big bang *which goes like when the time begins and the time is 10^{-43} secondsand the cosmos goes through super inflation which led to the expansion of an atom to the size of a grapefruit after that at 10^{-32} second post inflation the temperature was 10^{27} degree celsius and a hot soup of electrons, quarks, and other particles were present. Then at 10^{-6} seconds, the temperature cools down to 10^{13} celsius, and the cooling permits quarks to plump into protons and neutrons. The time is 3min and the temperature is 10^8 degrees Celsius but the temperature is still too hot to form into atoms, charged electrons, and protons prevent light from shining. Thus the universe was a super hot fog. Slowly time passes and it's 300,000 years now and the temperature is 10,000 degrees celsius the electrons combine with protons and neutrons to form atoms mostly helium and hydrogen thus the light can finally shine now. Soon a billion years pass and the temperature is -200 degrees celsius and gravity makes hydrogen and helium gas coalesce to form the giant clouds that will become galaxies; smaller clumps of gas collapse to create the first stars. Now the current time where the temperature is -270 degrees celsius there are several galaxies and stars present in the universe. So this is how a universe is created but as we know there is more than one universe present so now we will understand how they will multiply. The multiplication* *process is easy*

This chart shows us how the universe was multiplied.

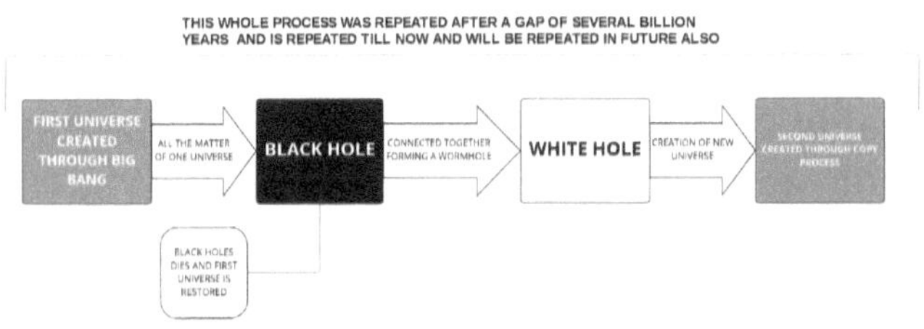

Enter Caption

It shows that several billion years after the first universe was created and fully developed. A black hole inside the universe had grown and had pulled many planets inside it. Still, it was growing bigger and bigger.

After several hundred billion years ago a black hole pulled 90% of the universe inside it.

Soon there was the birth of a white hole when the white hole and the black hole were connected. There was the birth of a wormhole which led to the transfer of matter from one bubble to another. Hence the white hole dies and the chains break now we have 2 universe bubbles one with matter and another one with matter and a black hole.

Slowly and slowly both of the universes develop and this cycle continues all the time in the simulation.

This is how multiple verses were created.

CHAPTER TWO

LIFE AND DEATH

As we got to know how the universe was created. Now several billion years later the planet earth was formed. Let's know where the human came from. First, it was a huge hot rocky sphere revolving around the sun. The temperature of the earth during that time was insanely high. Slowly the temperature starts to cool down when a huge bunch of asteroids strikes the planet earth. This was also called the late heavy bombardment which included precious asteroids that carried ice crystals with them. It helped in the formation of water bodies on the earth but still, there was no chance of life on earth. But soon there was an asteroid shower on earth again. Now, these asteroids carried high amounts of minerals, amino acids, carbon, and protein. As the earth was already covered with water the asteroids were capable of reaching the ocean bottoms. Whereas after several years, small bacteria

were formed, and this is how life began on earth. Soon the strength of these bacteria increased and small horses called <u>stromatolites</u> were formed. These stromatolites could perform <u>photosynthesis</u> due to which the amount of oxygen increased. As we know in the early stages there was no proper land area on the earth but later due to movement in tectonic plates the first supercontinent was formed named <u>Rodinia</u> which later broke down and there was a high amount of volcanic eruption due to which the amount of carbon dioxide rapidly increased. This carbon dioxide later forms clouds which lead to acid rain. Soon most of the carbon in the atmosphere came to the lithosphere with rain which resulted in the reduction of carbon in the environment. Soon came the first and longest ice age but later this ice age ended with a volcanic eruption resulting in the glaciers melting. But after that many different types of organisms were present in the sea including <u>Anomalocaris</u>, Pikia, etc. <u>Pikia</u> was the first organism to have a spinal cord. Later an organism named <u>Tiktaalik</u> became the first to walk on land; after further evolution, they were named <u>Tetrapods</u>. These Tetrapods were able to fully function on land.

Soon due to volcanic eruptions the temperature rose quickly and many species *of organisms died whereas some started to live underground to protect themselves from heat. Later the circumstances were restored and due to shifts in tectonic plates, a new supercontinent called <u>Pangea</u> was created. <u>Dinosaurs</u> evolved and the Earth was full of different species of dinosaurs but with dinosaurs, a small type of organism was also present on Earth called <u>mammals</u>. These mammals were very small in size and looked like <u>modern-day mice.</u> We all know later due to a meteorite all the dinosaurs became extinct and the main cause of extinction was <u>high temperature and explosion</u>. This was a great opportunity for leftover mammals which were small and lived underground. These mammals started eating dinosaur flesh for survival. Later Earth's condition was restored and mammals evolved. They evolved into different species of monkeys according to the conditions of their habitat. Again a shift in tectonic plates caused movement and the world took the shape we see now. Later, due to the creation of the East African Rift, the valley acted as a wall that prevented the entry of monsoon winds due to which the temperature in Africa rose and apes living there had to move down from trees and search for food and shelter. This is how evolution took place. Later they travelled places and started to live in groups and become more intelligent and they were called <u>Homoerectus</u>. Further evolution caused these* *species to become more intelligent and finally, we are here <u>Homosapiens</u>.*

BUT HAVE YOU WONDERED WHAT'S MISSING?

The theories of god and religion and the circle of life and death

When humans started to live in tribes and groups, the rulers or the leaders needed something to keep their people in law and order. They wanted a permanent answer to the question of the ordinary. So these leaders created an imaginary thing called GOD and to keep people together a RELIGION was created. This thing happened in almost every part of the world. That's why we have roughly <u>4200 religions and 18,000 estimated gods</u>. These will continue to expand according to further needs.

All perception of god, religion, life, and death was created

But the truth is every organism on earth or in the universe is immortal we can't be removed from existence

We all are made of molecules that cannot be destroyed

For example- Let's say a human body is made of 1000 molecules. The body is working when these 1000 molecules are joined correctly and we don't die, the formation just breaks apart.

This is a simulation and will continue forever...

CHAPTER THREE

REBIRTH

In the last chapter, we got to know about how the Earth was formed and what's the whole concept of life and death.

But everyone is confused about what is afterlife and rebirth.

Afterlife is said to be the life after death in religions they say that the souls go to heaven or hell but

The truth is there is no afterlife the molecules just break apart and remain on earth

There are many chances we can take rebirth and there are two types of rebirth.

The first one is Partial rebirth which occurs after the break of the formation of 1000 molecules and in this formation of 1000 molecules, 700 is the vessel, and 300 is energy. So when this formation is broken the vessel of 700 molecules is dismantled but that 300 energy is still traveling. Now to be conscious of this energy needs a vessel to work appropriately so in case this energy finds a new vessel we can consider it as a partial rebirth and the things associated with partial rebirth can be

1.

Memories

2.

Intellect

Where the new vessel can acquire old memories and intellect

Now comes the full rebirth which is the rarest process. In this process, after the molecular formation is dismantled but due to a coincidence, the 1000 molecules come in the same formation that was earlier the organism can be back and all the physical features, intellect, and memories are restored. In this process, it doesn't matter how many years before the molecular formation was dismantled, they just need to come in some form to achieve full rebirth.

CHAPTER FOUR

EMOTIONS

Emotion is a thing that has been with humans since their evolution. Emotions are the neurophysiological changes that are related to behavioural responses, feelings, thoughts, pleasure, and displeasure. There are a variety of emotions, for example, happiness, greed, revenge, etc. But the question arises: Do we need emotions? or Do we perceive emotions correctly?

We perceive emotions according to our tendency. It depends upon the environment, mindset, and various other factors. Hence every human being has a different way of perceiving things for example A person named

X was happy when his mother died whereas a person named Y was sad when his mother died, so here there can be many different reasons why X was happy and Y was sad.

There is also a saying that "we need to know the true meaning of a certain emotion to use it in the right place"

Let's say Happiness which seems like a positive emotion to a lot of people but the reality is when you are always happy in your current position 90% of the time you won't have the urge to grow. Happiness kills growth like this. Many other emotions which seem to be positive are negative and emotions which seem to be negative are positive.

Greed is a commonly identified negative emotion but actually, greed is one of the emotions that help humans to urge for more hence improving the growth rate of a human being.

If we just observe then we can see that most of our life, our behaviour is affected by these emotions which can create unwanted surroundings eventually leading to destruction.

Just imagine a world without emotions. Everything will go in order. Humans will be at their peak of productivity leading to the advancement of human society.

Hence, we all should go on this path for achieving our highest potential.

CHAPTER FIVE

BE COLD HEARTED

In the previous chapter, we discussed what will happen if humans were emotionless

There are several ways by which you can achieve emotionless behaviour

- *Let go of past emotions- There are several emotions that one never healed from and they repeatedly play in one's head. This emotional debt can hold a person back and influence one's life.*

- *Stop setting specific expectations- When a person doesn't act as you expect can cause a certain kind of emotional pain which can* be avoided by not setting an expectation

-

Keeping yourself busy- When one is goal-directed the energy is used to do activities that promote the goals rather than getting wasted on useless emotions.

-

Keep relationships on your terms- Avoid letting people get too close to you or control you. Define the type of relationships you want to be in.

-

Know what your goals are- When you know your destination it's hard for others to convince and control you.

-

Communicate your goals- Communicate exactly what you want and expect those things around you. Never compromise on your goals.

-

Say "NO" to anything that doesn't benefit you- Most of the time people agree to things they don't want just to fit in and after that, they end up with a loss. So it's better to say no to things

-

<u>*Contemplate the motives of other people*</u>*-When someone asks you a favor or help just analyze why that person is asking you and what will be your benefit for doing that work.*

•

<u>*Constantly build support systems*</u>*- When something mishappens you should always have a backup for it that is why it is suggested to have various support systems so that even if one backs off you have other ones to support you.*

These are some of the ways by which one can be Cold-hearted and become limitless. These things can help you build a strong personality and help you get what you want without wasting much time.

CHAPTER SIX

THE ENLIGHTEN NATIONS

Whenever we talk about a god we see a supreme identity that intelligent beings created to trap you inside an illusion But not everyone remains trapped around this illusion many people break free.

To be free from this illusion one must enlighten oneself. People including Gautam Buddha wanted enlightenment from the world for which he meditated for years but lately, his ways were considered a religion which is a false belief.

Similarly, Adam Weishaupt, founder of the Illuminati wanted to create such a society that will help multiple people to break free from this illusion. He was opposed by

Catholics because they didn't want people to break free. All they wanted was that people should remain under the control of their illusion. The Illuminati was opposed and was given the title of devil worshipper by the Catholics.

This was a common way of how powerful forces don't want anyone to leave the illusion. Unlike Illuminati and Gautam Buddha, there were many people who wanted to guide society and make people enlighten but were pushed down by the illusion creators.

Hence for a man to get enlightened one must believe that there is nothing above one's own consciousness and self.

This belief can create a feeling of superiority among people which will guide them to do more of what they are doing now. Eventually, this can help societies to run and function better. Observers will be able to see more development in almost all the streams. The amount of growth that will occur would be unbelievable.

CHAPTER SEVEN

THE 5 CURRENCIES

For Common people, there is only One currency which can be money or the currency of their home country but if we look closely they are 5 currencies that one must earn in order to be powerful

I) <u>Time</u>- One of the most important currencies of the wealthy. Everything in the world needs time. Your money, intelligence, and networks are worth nothing without proper time given to anything. Everything depends on how you utilise your time and the other 4 currencies also depend on your time.

II) <u>Thoughts</u>- Your thoughts nourish your brain. They tell you how you should behave and act in various situations. The thoughts are so powerful that a thought today which is worked upon can change your tomorrow. If you can control your thoughts and the way you think then a human's potential is limitless.

III) Intelligence- Your intelligence is your currency which no one else can take from you. Intelligence determines your potential the way you act on your thoughts and how efficiently you utilise your time. So always make sure to utilize your intellect at the right place.

IV) <u>Network</u>- We have always heard people say that your present is always influenced by your network. A person should build a network that can help him/her achieve a certain type of goal. The better and vast your network is, the more efficiently you can work towards a goal.

V) Money- The last currency is money as we know a person needs money for each and everything whereas even if a man loses his money but still has the other 4 currencies then it's not tough for him to generate the wealth again. Money plays an important role in one's life hence it can also influence a person's networks and help a person achieve a goal.

These were the 5 currencies that one should work on and if a person maintains a balance between all these then no one can stop that individual to get peace and success in life.

25

CHAPTER EIGHT

IMPORTANCE OF INFLUENCING

The word Influence means to affect the character of an individual. Influencing is an art and the one who knows how to utilize this art is capable of making his dreams come true.

Just imagine If you have certain ideas in your mind and you can influence people with your ideas there is a large probability that you can make those ideas come true and the reason behind this is that those people you influenced work together to achieve a certain goal.

There are only 3 ways by which one can be influenced and included-

I) <u>The Logic</u> - *If you can logically prove something to an individual there is a high probability that the person is going to believe in the theory you said can help you with your ideas. To Logically influence someone you must be confident and have your logic clear to you so you can push it on the other person.*

II) The Emotion- *The second way to influence someone is by using emotions. This can be done by having an emotional attachment with an individual and then taking his/her help to fulfill your own motives. Emotional influencing can also be done by Guilt trips and many other dark methods.*

III) The Power - *If you have a certain level of power and position then people will probably follow your orders and work according to you. It can be because of respect for the position or fear.*

These are the 3 ways by which a person can influence other people to full fill certain goals.

One should always work on this skill and try to improve his/her art of influencing.

The Enigmatic Thought

"The more and more darkness an individual fills in the life of his own the more and more he is moving towards unlocking the ability to see in the dark"

The Enigmatic Thoughts

"If you deeply look around yourself you will notice a pile of Dead Bodies which represents your unfulfilled Desires whose guilt will kill you soon"

www.ingramcontent.com/pod-product-compliance
Lightning Source LLC
Chambersburg PA
CBHW031248130726
47988CB00008B/3297